NANA BOOZHOO
OJIBWE WORDS AND PHRASES

(C)2017 MICHAEL LYONS

CONTENTS

PG 3:   HOW TO PRONOUNCE OJIBWE WORDS

PG: 4:   GREETINGS AND WEATHER

PG: 5:   TIME AND WEATHER

PG 6:   PAST AND FUTURE

PG 7:   YES OR NO WEATHER

PG 8:   QUESTIONS AND PHRASES

PG 9:   FEELINGS AND EMOTIONS

PG 10:   THIS AND THAT

PG 11:   COMMANDS

PG 12:   LET'S AND DON'T AND NAMES

PG 13:   ALL MY RELATIONS

PG 14:   WORK AND HOME

PG 16:   CONVERSATION QUESTIONS AND ACTIONS AND ARRIVAL

PG 18:   ANIMALS

PG 20:   NUMBERS

PG 21:   MONTHS

PG 22:   DAYS OF THE WEEK AND BODY PARTS

PG 23:   OTHER

PG 24:   RESERVATIONS

In loving memory of my grandma, Leona Lyons

HOW TO PRONOUNCE OJIBWE WORDS:

"Zh"- sounds like the "su" in *measure*

"a"- sounds like the "u" in *sun*

"aa"- sounds like the "a" in *father*

"i"- sounds like the "i" in *sit*

"ii"- sounds like the "ee" in *feet*

"o"- sounds like the "o" in *go*

"oo"- sounds like the "oo" in *food*

"e"- sounds like the "ay" in *stay*

GREETINGS

Boozhoo - "Hello"

Aaniin - "Hi, How are you? How are things?"

Nimino-ayaa - "I'm well, I'm fine."

Giin dash? - "And you."

Miigwech - "Thank you."

Giga-waabamin minawaa - "I'll see you again."

Giga-waabamin naagaj - "See you later"

Giga-waabamininim minawaa - "I'll see you people again."

Gichi - "Great"

Manidoo - "Spirit"

WEATHER

Mino-giizhigad - It is a good day.

Mino-giizhigan - It is a good day.

Gimiwan - It is raining.

Gichi-gimiwan - It is raining hard.

Zoogipon - It is snowing.

Gichi-zoogipon - It is snowing hard.

Noodin - It is windy.

Gichi-noodin - It is very windy.

Gizhide - It is hot.

Gichi-gizhide - It is very hot.

Gisinaa - It is cold.

Gichi-gisinaa - It is very cold.

Zaagaate - It is sunny.

Gichi-zaagaate - It is very sunny.

Ningwaakod - It is cloudy.

Gichi-ningwaakod - It is very cloudy.

A cool wind- **Dakaasin**

Clear- **Mizhakwad**

Cloudy- **Ningwaanakwad**

Foggy- **Awan**

It Freezes Over(lake)- **Gashkadin**

Nasty Weather- **Niiskaadad**

Slippery- **Ozhaashaa**

There are Northern Lights- Waawaate

There is a tornado or whilrwind- **Ashibishidosh**

Thundering- **Animikiikaa**

Warm and mild- **Aabawaa**

Windy- **Noodin**

It is·

TIME AND THE WEATHER

noongom - today, now

waabang - tomorrow

bijiinaago - yesterday

dibikong - last night

dibikak - this night (which will be)

megwaa, or **mego** - now; when; at the time when

geyaabi - still

maagizha - maybe

aazha - yet

PAST AND FUTURE TENSE

Gii-gimiwan - It rained.

Gii-zoogipon - It snowed.

Gii-gisinaa - It was cold.

Wii-mino-giizhigad - It is going to be a good day.

Wii-mino-gizhide - It is going to be hot.

Wii-gimiwan - It is going to rain.

Da-gimiwan - It will rain.

Wii-gimiwan waabang - It is going to rain tomorrow.

Da-gimiwan waabang - It will rain tomorrow.

Gii-gimiwan noongom - It rained today.

Gii-mino-giizhigad bijiinaago - It was a good day yesterday.

Gii-zoogipon bijiinaago - It snowed yesterday.

Gii-gimiwan bijiinaago - It rained yesterday.

Gii-gimiwan dibikong - It rain last night.

Gimiwan minawaa - It is raining again.

Geyaabi gimiwan - It is still raining.

Megwaa gimiwan - It is raining now.

Mego gimiwan - It is raining now.

Maagizha da-zaagaate waabang - Maybe it will be sunny tomorrow.

Aazha gimiwan - It is already raining.

Gii-gimiwan aazha - It rained already.

Wii-zoogipon dibikak - It is going to snow tonight.

Gimiwan na? - Is it raining?

Gimiwan na megwaa? - Is it raining right now?

Gimiwan na mego? - Is it raining right now?

Miinange - Yes. Of course.

Ehe - Yeah. Uh huh.

Zoogipon na? - Is it snowing?

Gaawiin - No.

Aaniin ezhiwebag? - How is the weather?

Aaniin ezhiwebag aagojing? - How is the weather outside?

Aaniin gaa-ezhiwebag bijiinaago? - How was the weather yesterday?

Aaniin ge-ezhiwebag waabang? - How will the weather be tomorrow?

Gaawiin ningikendanziin - I don't know.

Amanji sa - I don't know.

Gii-zoogipon na bijiinago? - Did it snow yesterday?

Gii-booni-gimiwan bijiinago? - It stopped raining yesterday.

Da-booni-gimiwan wiiba - It will stop raining soon.

Wii-maajii-gimiwan waabang - It is going to start to rain tomorrow.

Gii-booni-noodin - The wind stopped.

Gii-maajii-noodin - The wind started.

Do you remember?- Gimikwenden ina?

What are you doing? - Aaniin ezhichigeyand?

Nothing - Gaawiin gegoo

And you? - Giin-dash?

How are you?- Aaniin ezhi-ayaayan?

How is it outside?- Aaniin ezhiwebak agwajiing?

What are you called(name)?- Aaniin ezhinikaazoyan?

Where are you from?- Aandi wenjibaayan?

Where are you going?- Aandi ezhaayan?

Come here!- Ondaas

Come in- Bendigen

Hurry up - Wewiib

Wait - Beka

Please- Daga

Say it again(repeat)- Ikidon miinawaa

FEELINGS

Nishkaadizi - "S/he is angry."

Menwendam - "S/he is happy."

Bakade - "S/he is hungry.

Maanendam - "S/he is sad"

Aakozi - "S/he is sick."

Mino-giizigad - "It is a good day."

Gimiwan - "It is raining."

Zoogipon - "It is snowing."

Noodin - "It is windy."

Gizhide - "It is hot."

Gisinaa - "It is cold."

Waaseyaa - "It is sunny."

Ningwaakod - "It is cloudy."

EMOTIONS

I am…

Afraid- Ningotaaj

Cold- Ningiikaj

Crazy- Ningiiwanaadiz

Hungry- Nimbakade

Mad- Ninishkaadiz

Resting- Nindanweb

Sad- Ningashkendam

Sick- Nindaakoz

Sorry- Nimaanendam

Thirsty- Ninoondeminikwe

Tired- Nindayekoz

Warm- Ningiizhooz

Well- Nimino-ayaa

Working- Nindanokii

THIS AND THAT

Wegonen owe? - What is this?
Wegonen iwe? - What is that?

Wegonen iwedi? - What is that over there?

Awenen wa'a? - Who is this?

Awenen awe? - Who is that?

Awenen awedi? - Who is that over there?

Oginiig iwe - That is a rose.

Mitig awe - That is a tree.

Nibi iwe - That is water.

Ishgode owe - This is fire.

Mazina'igan iwe - That is a book.

Adoopowin owe - This is a table.

Inini wa'a - This is a man.

Inini awe - That is a man.

Inini awedi - that is a man over there.

Ikwe awe - That is a woman.

Giizis awe - That is the sun.

Dibiki-giizis awe - That is the moon

Awenen awe inini? - Who is that man?

Awenen awe ikwe? - Who is that woman?

Awenen awe gwiiwizenz? - Who is that boy?

Awenen awe ikwizenz? - Who is that girl?

Nibaabaa awe - That is my father.

Nimaamaa awe - That is my mother.

Ningozis awe - That is my son.

Nindaanis awe - That is my daughter.

Animosh na awe? - Is that a dog?

Inini na awe? - Is that a man?

Mazina'igan na owe? - Is that a book?

Mazina'igan na iwe? - Is that a book?

Aambe - Come on, Come here.

Biindigen - Enter, Go inside.

Biindigeg - Enter, Go inside you people.

Abin - Sit.

Abig - Sit you people.

Namadabin - Sit down.

Namadabig - Sit down you people.

Wiisinin - Eat.

Wiisinig - Eat you people.

Zaagaan - Go outside.

Zaagaamog - Go outside you people.

Giiwen - Go home.

Giiweg - Go home you people.

Maajaan - Leave, Go.

Maajaag - Leave, Go you people.

Ikidon - Say it.

Ikidog - Say it you people.

Bi-giiwen - Come home.

Bi-giiweg - come home you people.

Bi-wiisinin - Come eat.

Bi-wiisinig - Come eat you people.

Ando-abin - Go sit.

Ando-abig - Go sit you people.

Ando-namadabin - Go sit down.

Ando-namadabig - Go sit down you people.

Ando-wiisinin - Go eat.

Ando-wiisinig - Go eat you people.

Booni-wiisinin - Stop eating.

Booni-wiisinig - Stop eating you people.

Ikidon minawaa - Say it again.

Ikidog minawaa - Say it again you people.

Wiisinidaa - Let's eat.

Biindigedaa - Let's go inside.

Zaagaandaa - Let's go outside.

Giiwedaa - Let's go home.

Maajaadaa - Let's leave

Gego biindigeken - Don't enter.

Gego biindigekeg - Don't enter you people.

Gego zaaganken - Don't go outside.

Gego zaagankeg - Don't go outside you people.

NAMES

Aaniin ezhinikaazoyan? - What is your name?

Aubrey nindizhinikaaz - Aubrey is my name.

Aubrey na gidizhnikaaz? -Is Aubrey your name?

Aaniin ezhinikaazod awe inini? - What is that man's name?

Aaniin ezhinikaazod? - What is his/her name?

Aubrey izhinikaazo - Aubrey is his name.

Aaniin ezinikaazod gimaamaa? - What is your mother's name?

Ann izhinikaazo nimaamaa. - Ann is my mother's name.

Gaawiin Agnes izhinikaazosii - Her name is not Agnes.

Gaawiin John nindizhinikaazosii - My name is not John.

ALL MY RELATIONS

Nibaabaa - My father

Gibaabaa - Your father

Obaabaayan - His/her father

Nimaamaa - My mother

Gimaamaa - Your mother

Omaamaayan - His/her mother

Ningozis - My son

Ningozisag - My sons

Gigozis - Your son

Gigozisag - Your sons

Ogozisan - His/her son

Ogozisa' - His/her sons

Nindaanis - My daughter

Nindaanisag - My daughters

Gidaanis - Your daughter

Gidaanisag - Your daughters

Odaanisan - His/her daughter

Odaanisa' - His/her daughters

Nisaye - My older brother

Nisayeyag - My older brothers

Gisaye - Your older brother

Gisayeyag - Your older brothers

Osayeyan - His/her older brother

Osayeya' - His/her older brothers

Nimise - My older sister

Nimiseyag - My older sisters

Gimisa - Your older sister

Gimiseyag - Your older sisters

Omiseyan - His/her older sister

Omiseya' - His/her older sisters

Nishiime - My younger sibling

Nishiimeyag - My younger siblings

Gishiime - Your younger sibling

Gishiimeyag - Your younger siblings

Oshiimeyan - His/her younger sibling

Oshimeya' - His/her younger sibling

Gidanokii na? - Are you working?

Gidanokii na mego? - Are you working right now?

Nindanokii - I'm working

Nisaye anokii - My older brother is working.

Anokii - S/he is working.

Noongom anokii nimbaabaa - My father is working

Nisayeyag anokiiwag - My older brothers are working.

Anokiiwag - They are working.

Gigii-anokii na bijiinaago? - Did you work yesterday?

Gaawiin ningii-anokiisii - I didn't work.

Gii-anokii na gibaabaa? - Did you father work?

Gaawiin gii-anokiisii - S/He didn't work.

Gisayeyag na gii-anokiiwag bijiinaago? - Did you older brothers work yesterday?

Gaawiin gii-anokiisiiwag - They didn't work.

Giwii-ando-anokii na waabang? - Are you going to work tomorrow?

Gigii-ando-anokii na bijiinaago? - Did you go ti work yesterday?

Gaawiin niwii-ando-anokiisii noongom - I'm not going to work today.

Giga-ayab na waabang? - Will you be **home tomorrow?**

Gigii-ayab na bijiinaago? - Were you home yesterday?

Gimaamaa na gii-ayabi bijiinago? - Was your mother home yesterday?

Da-ayabi na waabang? - Will she be home tomorrow?

Mary na ayabi mego? - Is Mary home right now?

Ayabi - S/He is at home.

Nindayab - I am at home.

Gidayab - You are at home.

Gidani-giiwe na? - Are you going home?

Nindani-giiwe - I am going home.

Giwii-giiwe na? - Are you going to go home?

Giwii-giiwe na waabang? - Are you going to go home tomorrow?

Niwii-giiwe - I am going to go home.

Niwii-giiwe zhemaag - I am going to go home immediately.

Wii-giiwe awe ikwe - This woman is going to go home.

Wii-ani-giiwe - S/He is going to go **home**.

Aazha ani-giiwe - S/He is already going home.

Gii-ani-giiwe na? - Did s/he go home?

Aazha gii-ani-giiwe - S/he already went home.

Ningii-giiwe bijiinaago - I went home yesterday.

Niwii-giiwe waabang - I am going to go home tomorrow.

Gibi-giiwe na? - Are you coming home?

Gii-bi-giiwe na? - Did s/he come home?

Ayabi na aazha? - Is s/he home already?

Joe bi-giiwe - Joe is coming home.

Aaniin ekidoyan? - What did you just say?

"Wegonen iwe" nindikid - 'What is that' I said.

Aaniin gaa-ikidod awe inini? - What did that man say?

"Ambe omaa" gii-ikido - 'Come here' he said.

Aaniin gaa-ikidoyan? - What did you say a while ago?

Aaniin waa-ikidoyan? - What are you going to say?

Aaniin ge-ikidoyan? - What will you say?

Biindige - S/He just went inside.

Gii-biindige - S/He went inside.

Wii-biindige - S/He is going to go inside.

Da-biindige - S/He will go inside.

Zaagaam - S/He just went outside.

Gii-zaagaam - S/He went outside.

Wii-zaagaam - S/He is going to go outside.

Da-zaagaam - S/He will go outside.

Biindige gimaamaa - Your mother just went inside.

Daagoshin Joe - Joe just now arrived.

Maajaa - S/He just left.

Nisaye giimaajaa bijiinaago - My older brother left yesterday.

Zaagaamoog abinoojiyag - The children are going outside.

Bi-biindigewag - They are coming in.

Gii-daagoshinoog ogowe ininiwag dibikong - These men arrived last night.

Maagizha gii-biindigewag - Maybe they went inside.

Gii-ani-zaagaamoog na? - Did they go outside?

Aazha gii-zaagaamoog - They already went out.

Da-daagoshinoog ogowe ikwewag tibikak - These women will arrive tonight.

Nimbiindige - I am going inside.

Nizaagaam - I am going outside.

Nimaajaa - I am leaving.

Gigii-zaagaam na dibikong? - Did you go out(side) last night?

Ningii-maajaa bijiinaago - I left yesterday.

Ningii-daagoshin noomaya - I arrived a little while ago.

Ningii-daagoshin menwiinzha - I arrived long ago.

Giwii-maajaa na zemag? - Are you going to leave immediately?

Giga-bi-daagoshin na wiiba? - Will you arrive here soon?

Ninga-maajaa waabang - I'll leave tomorrow.

Gaawiin Joe wii-zaagaanzii - Joe doesn't want to go outside.

Gaawiin abinoojiyag gii-maajaasiiwag - The children didn't leave (some time ago).

Gaawiin niwii-biindigesii - I am not going to go inside.

Gaawiin ningii-daagoshininzii bijiinaago - I didn't arrive yesterday.

ANIMALS

Ant(s)- **Enigoons(ag)**	Chicken(s)- **Baaka' aakwe(yag)**
Bass(s)- **Ashigan(ag)**	Chipmunk(s)- **Agongosens(ag)**
Bear(s)- **Makwa(g)**	Coyote(s)- **Wiisagi-ma' iingan(ag)**
Beaver(s)- **Amik(wag)**	Cow(s)- **Bizhiki(wag)**
Bee(s)- **Aamoo(g)**	Crane(s)- **Mooshka' oosi(wag)**
Bird(s)- **Bineshii(yag)**	Crow(s)- **Aandeg(wag)**
Blackbird(s)- **Asiginaak(wag)**	Deer(s)- **Waawaashkeshi(wag)**
Bluejay(s)- **Diindiisi(wag)**	Dog(s)- **Animosh(ag)**
Bobcat(s)- **Gidagaa-bizhiw(ag)**	Dragonfly(ies)- **Boochikwanishi(wag)**
Butterfly(s)- **Memengwaa(g)**	Duck(s)- **Zhiishiib(ag)**
Buffalo(s)- **Mashkodebizhiki(wag)**	Bald Eagle(s)- **Migizi(wag)**
Cat(s)- **Gaazhagens(ag)**	Golden Eagle(s)- **Giniw(ag)**
Chickadee(s)- **Gijigaaneshii(yag)**	Firefly(ies)- **Waawaatesi(wag)**

Fish(s)- **Giigoo(yag)**

Fly(ies)- **Ojiins(ag)**

Fox(es)- **Waagosh(ag)**

Frog(s)- **Omakakii(g)**

Canadian Goose(geese)- **Nika(g)**

Snow Goose(geese)- **Wewe(g)**

Hawk(s)- **Gekek(wag)**

Horse(s)- **Bebezhigooganzhii(g)**

Hummingbird(s)- **Nenookaasi(wag)**

Loon(s)- **Maang(wag)**

Mallard(s)- **Aninshib(ag)**

Marten(s)- **Waabizheshi(wag)**

Mink(s)- **Zhaangweshi(wag)**

Minnow(s)- **Giigoozens(ag)**

Moose(s)- **Mooz(oog)**

Mosquito(s)- **Zagime(g)**

Mouse(mice)- **Waawaabigonoojii(yag)**

Muskrat(s)- **Wazhashk(wag)**

Northern Pike(s)- **Ginoozhe(g)**

Oriole(s)- **Asiginaak(wag)**

Owl(s)- **Gookooko' oo(g)**

Otter(s)- **Nigig(wag)**

Partridge(s)- **Bine(wag)**

Pheasant(s)- **Mayagi-bine(wag)**

Pig(s)- **Gookoosh(ag)**

Porcupine(s)- **Gaag(wag)**

Rabbit(s)- **Waabooz(oog)**

Raccoon(s)- **Esiban(ag)**

Robin(s)- **Opichi(wag)**

Skunk(s)- **Zhigaag(wag)**

Sparrow(s)- **Gakaashkinejii(wag)**

Spider(s)- **Asabikeshii(yag)**

Squirrel(s)- **Ajidamoo(g)**

Snake(s)- **Ginebig(oog)**

Painted turtle(s)- **Miskwaadesi(wag)**

Snapping turtle(s)- **Mikinaak(wag)**

Sturgeon(s)- **Name(wag)**

Sucker(s)- **Namebin(ag)**

Sunfish(s)- **Agwadaashi(wag)**

Thunderbird(s)- **Binesi(wag)**

Turkey(s)- **Mizise(g)**

Turtle(s)- **Mishiike(yag)**

Vulture(s)- **Wiinaange(wag)**

Walleye(s)- **Ogaa(wag)**

Weasel(s)- **Zhingos(ag)**

Whitefish(s)- **Adikameg(wag)**

Wolf(wolves)- **Ma' iingan(ag)**

Woodchuck(s)- **Makakojiishi(wag)**

Downey Woodpecker(s)-
Baapaase(wag)

Pileated Woodpecker(s)- **Meme(g)**

Woodtick(s)- **Ezigaa(g)**

Wren(s)- **Anaamisagadaweshii(wag**

NUMBERS

One- **Bizhig**

Two- **Niizh**

Three- **Niswi**

Four- **Niiwin**

Five- **Naanan**

Six- **Ningodwaaswi**

Seven- **Niizhwaaswi**

Eight- **Nishwaaswi**

Nine- **Zhaangaswi**

Ten- **Midaaswi**

Eleven to nineteen add Ashi before number

Eleven- **Ashi bezhig**

Twenty to twenty-nine add **Niizhtana ashi** before number

Twenty-one- **Niizhtana ashi bezhig**

Thirty to thirty-nine add **Nisimidana ashi**

Thirty-one- **Nisimidana ashi bezhig**

Forties add **Niimidana ashi**

Forty-one- **Niimidana ashi bezhig**

Fifties add **Naanimidana ashi**

Fifty-one- **Naanimidana ashi bezhig**

Sixties add **Ningodwaasimidana ashi**

Seventies add **Niizhwaasimidana ashi**

Eighties add **Nishwaasimidana ashi**

Nineties add **Zhaangasimidana ashi**

Hundreds add **Ningodwaak ashi**

MONTHS

January(Great Spirit Moon)- **Gichi-Manidoo-Giizis**

February(Sucker Fish Moon)- **Namebini-Giizis**

March(Crust on the Snow Moon)- **Onaabani-Giizis**

April(Sap Boiling Moon)- **Iskigamizige-Giizis**

May(Flower Budding Moon)- **Zaagibagaa-Giizis**

June(Strawberry Moon)- **Ode' imini-Giizis**

July(Half -Way, Summer Moon)- **Abitaa-Niibini-Giizis**

August(Wild Rice Moon)- **Manoominike-Giizis**

September(Leaves Changing Color Moon)- **Waatebagaa-Giizis**

October(Leaves Falling Moon)- **Binaakwe-Giizis**

November(Freezing Over Moon)- **Gashkadino-Giizis**

December(Little Spirit Moon)- **Manidoo-Giizisoons**

DAYS OF THE WEEK

Monday(day after prayer day)- **Ishwaa-anami'e giizhigad**

Tuesday(second day)- **Niizho-giizhigad**

Wednesday(half way)- **Aabitoose**

Thursday(fourth day)- **Niiyo giizhigad**

Friday(fifth day)- **Naano giizhigad**

Saturday(floor washing day)- **Giziibiigiisaginige-giizhigad**

Sunday(prayer day)- **Anami'e-giizhigad**

BODY PARTS

Arm(s)- **Ninik(an)**

Back(s)- **Nipikwan(an)**

Ear(s)- **Nitawag(an)**

Eye(s)- **Nishkiinzhig(oon)**

Finger(s)- **Nininjiins(an)**

Foot(feet)- **Ninzid(an)**

Head(s)- **Nishtigwaan(an)**

Heart(s)- **Ninde'(an)**

Hand(s)- **Ninij(iin)**

Leg(s)- **Nikaad(an)**

Mouth(s)- **Nindoon(an)**

Nose(s)- **Injaanzh(an)**

Stomach(s)- **Nimsad(an)**

Toe(s)- **Niibinaakwaanizidaan(an)**

Tongue(s)- **Nindenaniw(an)**

Birch bark- **Wiigwaas**

Blanket(s)- **Waabooyaan(an)**

Casino-**Endazhi-ataading**

College(s)- **Gabe-gikendaasoowigamig**

Dancers- **Naamiwaad**

Day- **Giizhigad**

Drink- **Minikwe**

Drum(s)- **Dewe'igan(ag)**

Earth- **Aki**

Eat- **Wiisini**

Feather(s)- **Miigwan(ag)**

Gas Station- **Waasamoobimide-adaawewigamig**

Hospital- **Aakoziiwigamig**

Lake(s)- **Zaaga'igan(an)**

Medicine Man- **Mashkikiiwinini**

Medicine Woman- **Mashkikiikwe**

Money- **Zhooniyaa**

Moon(s)- **Dibiki-giizis(oog)**

Night- **Dibikad**

No- **Gaawiin**

Ojibwe people(s)- **Anishinaabe(g)**

Ojibwe language- **Anishinaabemowin**

Outside- **Agwajiing**

Pipe(s)- **Opwaagan(ag)**

Powwow- **Niimi'idim**

Restaurant- **Wiisiniiwigamig**

River(s)- **Ziibi(wan)**

School- **Gikinoo'amaadiiwigamig**

Singers- **Negamowaad**

Smudge-**Nookwezigan**

Star(s)- **Anang(oog)**

Store- **Adaawewigamig**

Stream(s)- **Ziibiins(an)**

Sun- **Giizis**

Sunset- **Bangishimog**

Today(now)- **Noongom**

Tonight- **Noongom dibikad**

Town(s)- **Oodena(wan)**

Warrior(s)- **Ogichidaa(wag)**

Yes- **Eya'**

Bad River- **Mashkii-ziibing**

Bay Mills- **Gnoozhekaaning**

Fond du Lac- **Nagaajiwanaang**

Grand Portage- **Gichi-Oniigaming**

Keewenaw Bay- **Wiikwedong**

Lac Courte Oreilles- **Odaawaa-zaaga'iganiing**

Lac du Flambeau- **Waaswaaganing**

Lac Vieux Desert- **Getegitigaaning**

Leech Lake- **Gaa-Zagaskwaajimekaag**

MilleLacs Lake- **Misi-Zaaga'igaaning**

Nett Lake- **Asabiikone-Zaaga'iganing**

Red Cliff- **Gaa-Miskwaabikaag**

Red Lake- **Miskwaagamiiwi-Zaaga'iganing**

Mole Lake- **Zaka'aaganing**

Sault Ste Marie- **Baawitigong**

Vermilion Lake- **Onamani-Zaaga'iganing**

White Earth- **Gaa-Waabaabiganikaag**